~About the Cover~

Between Heaven and Earth a Mighty Rainbow is Beginning to Appear. It is as Bright as the Sun and is Powerful Sign and Signet of Our Love made Manifest. In the Age of Spiritual Enlightenment We Stand on the Foundation Stone, the Corner Stone of Our True Being. In One Hand is a Ruler to Measure Truth and in the Other We Extend Beauty. In Truth, Beauty and Freedom We Connect to the Very Heart of the Heavenly Realm and Our Love is Reflected Back to Us. The Age of Aquarius has Begun Bringing with it the Healing Waters of Life and Wisdom. The Earth is Born Anew Full of Bounty and Beauty.

~FORWARD~

We are entering into the Aquarian Age. This is a time when the outpouring of the Knowledge of Spirit will flow abundantly. In this book you will find 150 writings of affirmation and wisdom to guide you to fully embracing and dancing within this Age of Spiritual Freedom. Each writing is a reflection of the human condition. Through the spectrum of struggle to victory you will feel the connection for we are all one, each of us seeking peace and happiness. These writings came into creation as part of my morning meditation and devotion. Every morning I had one simple request... "To bring forth the highest and the best to be of the greatest benefit to all of Humanity." You may also wish to make these a part of your meditations or simply draw upon them "randomly" to nourish your soul. Feel free to substitute your Teachers, Guides or Masters names in place of words like *Mother/Father God* or *Divine Source*. All Paths lead to the One and All Paths are Holy when Pursued in Love. May this book be of Divine Service to this One that we may All find our way back Home to Love and Peace.

Love Illuminations: Aquarian Age Word of
Spiritual Freedom
Self Published
by
David Norman Christy Sr.
(under pen name David Shepard-Love)

For inquiries or to order additional copies of this
book contact
natureswheel@gmail.com
or
www.Amazon.com

Cover Art by Sharon Nichols
Cover Design by David Norman Christy Sr.

To My Loving Parents
Dorothy Shepard and John Love

To My Twin Flame for Showing Me
the Power of Love Illuminated

To All People Everywhere
for Their Yearning to Be Free

LOVE ILLUMINATIONS

Aquarian Age Word of Spiritual Freedom

TABLE OF CONTENTS

LOVE ILLUMINATIONS

~Day 1~
Day One

Within this book are words of Wisdom. Words of times and those that help us with our climb.

Bringing my heart to a center focus... Seeing the one light that burns brightly in the family of Human-Kind and Loving God, with all my Heart, Mind and Strength a resurrection of life will be mine.

Here I sit as one person with a plan and for the eternal moment of the now I know I am one with you because you too, love.

Peace be with you, my child, and you will find your "Pot of Gold" at the end of the Rainbow. I salute you and move into greater consciousness.

~~~~

~Day 2~
Your Ascension

On wings of silver my heart is lifted up to a place of the greatest. Up above this sweet earth I fly free and see and work with my "invisible" brothers and sisters.

They tell me, in order that I may pass it along, "Fear not, my beloved, you are becoming a child of the Universe and you know of the golden thread that unites all life."

Your ascension into heaven happens all the time you Love; for truly I say unto you, "God is Love. You are one with Love while maintaining the Divine Perspective."

The mortal of my body found its Freedom this day. In Light I Am.

~~~~

~Day 3~
Our Earthly Path

Into this world we are sent, caste into the form of Human and physical. We soon see at the instant of birth this encasement of flesh is a blessing. Then, with the introduction of pain, the illusion of the material world quickly begins to alter the perception of the spiritual reality we lost (in consciousness) during this "coming."

We now must earn our daily bread and find, while rising above temptations, happiness. We cross many rivers and think to ourselves, "Where is the time going?" "Which path leads me to where I need to go?"

Lost in the "searching for bread" you burn up many carnal experiences and yet it is going too fast. The rewards of heaven are not coming in this space as you (in self) would expect.

I cry out to you from the depths of my soul, "See the Signs!! Watch for those gates to heaven. They are around every corner. You can rise above the illusion of this world of pain and form!"

Reborn, you soar to the point of your origin to experience God and Love. Yes, in trust, it will all work out.

~~~~

~Day 4~
Take Wings

Life, as it would seem, has many ups and downs. We are caught on that "Merry-go-round;" bobbing up and down and going round and round, while all the time we have our mind's eye on the prize just beyond reach; limited by the physical.

If you would only see your "horse" not as attached and going round in circles, but instead, with wings of Freedom. Then in a harmonious balance of strength and grace you can fly.

All the prizes are yours, just take wings, my friend, and believe.... you will see.

~~~~

~Day 5~
Releasing Burdens

There comes a time in our life when the burdens of the past become so heavy we seem as a beast of burden, loaded to the hilt and trudging down the way we are told to go.

Many of the past "mis"-deeds of others and of self are still there... still not forgiven.

Some use a wagon to carry this burden; and while the load seems lighter it in reality gives it a chance to accumulate even more, while the burden remains ever attached.

Free yourself... Forgive your Brother and your Sister and especially Yourself, for it was you who decided to make it a burden in the first place.

As you Truly do this, from the Heart, your load will become lighter and with practice you will be as free as the birds and as mighty as Human-in-God can be.

Love Yourself.

~~~~

~Day 6~
A True Lover

Floating as a balloon I move freely across the space that encompasses me. I see the tears and the laughter of those around me; yet, by "Will," I choose to not take them in on an emotional level.

Feeling I pursue the path Divine Love would have me go down yet wondering in this do I close my eyes to the "feelings" of others? Still I know Divine Source lives in all. It is the light that shines upon all life in this world.

I, as a true lover of life, must be sensitive to expressions of all life forms and as God's reflection be in an non-changing state of love perfection, for Divine Source loves all the same.

Mother/Father God may not approve of one's action, yet, They could never influx Their being to love none-the-less. I am becoming as God everyday.

~~~~

~Day 7~
Power of Love

Moving into this new day; the first day of the rest of my life, I will look for and see Love-Light within everyone... making us all one.

I will, in the eternal now, also see this love-light burning bright within me and freely allow it to enlighten myself and others.

I come as a child of God this day, putting forth only my best, and expecting only the best from the totality of my environment. Today (All Times) I Know the Power of Love.

~~~~

~Day 8~
Reflecting Mother/Father God

It is preordained in the great Cosmos of space that we all will come to a point of truly loving ourselves. How would it be possible to love others while from this point the love starts is dingy and darkened by mistrust and guilt?

It has been said by many masters, "Come to know self, intimately, you will also come to know the secrets, for contained within your being is a portion of every part of this Great Universe."

You truly are Mother/Father God made manifest as a reflection of Their Being. Will you choose to reflect Them in your life... consciously? God is Love and God is Light; in Them there is no darkness at all.

By bringing your-self to a point of pure love all darkness will be dispelled. You will walk as Kings and Queens. The Garden of this New Age will bring you fruits of Happiness, prosperity and all Good... Simply Love Yourself.

~~~~

~Day 9~
Step Forward

As we look at our feet, a symbol for higher understanding can be realized. The feet are what carry us down the path toward enlightenment.

First in the mind and then in the heart the idea of movement is conceived, yet, here on a "human" level, an idea can become stagnant. An action is required... a step forward to allow this idea of creation to come into manifestation.

Within us also; as active "God/Human," is the ability to create by bringing our projections of creation into perfect alignment with the creative flow of God. Here... All movement is set into action.

Our feet, as symbols, find even a higher reality, saying, "You are the Creator, take the steps forward in alignment with the universal creator and the legions of heaven are at your command." So Be It!!

~~~~

~Day 10~
A New Way

Awake, you child of the universe!! See the light of the new day. Feel yourself a part of this new way, for truly you would not even exist if Mother/Father God did not have a divine purpose for you.

If you would merely open your eyes, then you would see. Open the sight to your heart and let the communication flow. Open the door to your mind and see the connection that makes you a great part of the higher reality.

Now is the time and you are the key to the blessed unfoldment of the New Age. Stand up in full power and take your well earned place at the right hand of God.

The love in your heart will light your way then you will know you are, "God, I Am."

~~~~

Illumined Purpose

There are loved ones in your life who have spent much of their years with you. You have seen them grow and at times it may seem slow.

In gratitude, you bless the grace of God as they go toward the way of the light, for now you know the truer purpose of their lives has been illumined.

It is a time of great singing in the heavens... as we all move into this great wonder-land of Freedom. In Commitment to your end of pure love all reality will flow into the river of life and there-in blend in the perfection of the one true Divine Source, which by choice, you have moved ever so sweetly into.

You are a divine creature because now you are one with Love Divine.

~~~~

~Day 12~
The Now

We live in the moment of the now... yet, in this body human we find ourselves counting the moments with desires in the past and the future. The "Now" of the here, under the condition of mortal, can not exist.

It is only by taking on the spirit of your being you begin to move beyond the limits of time; living not in the barriers you set up with your five senses, but truly experiencing the Now through your heart.

Here, as you process your environment, you will judge not, saying, "It is good or bad." You will know it for what it is and you will flow with the Living Spirit with it and within all.

Moving beyond time, in a space of no time, you allow grace to guide you. Counting of the moments no longer matters to you. You move freely as the Dove of Peace, always where you need to be... never early, never late. The spirit you have illumined with your heart is now your time-keeper.

In the silence of contemplation you give thanks to the creator...within and outside. You truly live in the eternal now; In grace.

~~~~

~Day 13~
Mountains of Life

Going high into the Mountains of Life I heard a voice from the Heavens say unto me, "Learn the lessons of life... Seek always peace first and your path will inevitably lead you to a Place of Happiness."

"As a brother would strike you; then, in turn, love him all the more. As one would take from you, give him double his bounty. You are to be his light, not his judge."

"In Divine attunement with the Living God of All you live the lesson of life's experiences to the fullest; always know and act as center in the trials for growth you are given."

Awake and rejuvenated on this glorious day, I came down from my refuge in the Mountains; placing myself in the illusion and pain of this world.

Now I would learn, see and experience the all-encompassing communication field, for now I see the light in all people and things and love them Freely.

Peace is mine this Day.

~~~~

~Day 14~
Love's Light

The light enfolds my being and instantly I soar up a spiraling shaft of white light. I move into a space of creation and see the movement of God-in-Action. Oh, the wonder of it.

Here, seeing the convergence of man and spirit, seeing the beauty of it, it becomes clear. We all move toward the light, for this light is the center of all light. Indeed, it is the Creator. It is Love.

Imagine It moving in your seamless white garment and finding your center and here; knowing It is love. Peace resounds in your heart and for an eternity as you recognize your connection with the Great omni-presence of Mother/Father God.

In recognition of this event you see; you and I are not alone. We have simply taken the course that all of humanity will take on their steps to God.

~~~~

~Day 15~
Morning Star

With the rising of the morning star you bring yourself from sleeping and greet the new day with centeredness and action toward bringing in the light of the world; allowing you to express it in its fullness.

You are floating as a blade of grass down the river of life... moving to where you need to go; in flow with all life around you. You realize you love yourself and see this love manifested in people and places you venture into.

Awakened from your sleep with a smile on your heart, you and Love Divine will never part. In truth, this is brought this day.

~~~~

Three-Fold Balance

Into this world you are sent from the realms of the spiritual. By choice, you have said, "Yes, I do want to descend into the physical plane of existence so that I may learn the totality of my being; to experience first hand, the denseness, while ever being attracted by the divine source I came from; the realm of the spirit."

Within you is the perfect three-fold balance of Human, God and Spirit. In your conscious mind the balance is what we all are working toward. Balance will be had by all. It was your choice to descend to the earth and now is the time to choose in the freedom of Love to ascend back into heaven.

Keep up, always do your best and know of your omnipotent power within. These are the keys to moving along the lighted path. Set goals for yourself and keep them, for you are a child of God and whatever you desire with all your heart, soul, mind and strength so shall it be done, By Grace.

~~~~

~Day 17~
Universal Presence

With thankfulness deep within our heart we stand together and honor the Creator. We see the light from within us become one with the light that flows in universal presence.

Mother/Father God, now awaken through our projection of gratitude, moves with Their entire being to bring about a change. Realization of the Power of Love is now made manifest. Oh, the glory of it, to see the light from the outside move to the center of all and in an instant transmute mortal into immortality.

The choice for you is quite simple, my sweet child. Be thankful, live with an attitude of gratitude and bow before the Creator. In light, you shall live forever.

~~~~

~Day 18~
Presence of Peace

Flowing Freely now shows me the way to drift. I become one with God and in grateful union we are now a plan set into action. A Presence of Peace on Earth is established.

First the Foundation Stone is secured, then this base structure of reality combines in perfect order with the Rainbow of Life. An infinite range of colors become defined. Humans view this and their hearts become one with the infinite nature of creation.

A key of Life is flowing from the center of the Being of Life. Love inspired, consciousness connected and light transforming... the full power of Will, magnified in Freedom, is Known. Resurrection of All life; for now the Divine Purpose has been revealed.

~~~~

~Day 19~
Special Days

Special days in one's life can help show the connections into higher reality On these days you find a reason, from your individual perspective, why they are special.

It is the relationship between time and space you see as unique. Nothing ever happens by accident. Always if you will open the eyes to the soul you will see. If you have a special date each month then set it aside knowing the Flow of Divine Source will bring you many signs and wonders. Know you will be shown that as you love and believe, you are Master and truly God-Empowered.

Supreme Bliss can be yours at any moment if by faith you know the sign is meant for you now. Believe and you shall be made whole and the heavens will be at your command.

~~~~

~Day 20~
The Least of These

There are children out there in the dark who are hungry. They toss and turn with pain in their stomachs and their hearts. While you, in your make-believe happiness, rationalize, "Oh, it's not all that bad."

Open your eves to the hunger of your own soul, for it, being one with all souls, is crying in the night and knowing what is right it moves you into a place where you must make a change.

Mother/Father God gave us free will yet our soul never operates independent of any other human soul. "As you do unto the least of these my brother and sisters you have also done it unto me. Give and you shall receive; take and it shall be taken from you."

Nothing is ever for Free, Only the Love from You and Me.

~~~~

~Day 21~
Our Mirror

The world is your mirror. If you can stand up to this mirror and see your reflection, the world, as beautiful, loving, kind, and compassionate, you will have created a beautiful, loving, kind and compassionate world. Yet, if through your eyes you see only hate, anger, and greed then this is also the world you create.

In the morning as you awaken for the new day look at yourself with all the loving aspects of Divine Source and truly see them. As you see with your mind and heart... So it will be... The World, the reflection of your being, will see you as lovely as you see yourself.

See the beauty of the Creator within and you can transform the world into a Garden of Flowing Peace.

~~~~

~Day 22~
Divine Heart Flow

Within this Divine Heart flows a river. A river that flows out from the perfection of Mother/Father God into the center of all life... Revitalizing all that is not in complete perfection and bringing about a clear channel for consciousness, the light of mind, to flow through.

Where there was death, there is now life. Where there was sorrow there is now happiness and for fear only Love Reigns Supreme.

You, in wondering, ask, "Why the change?" Acting from the very center of your being the answer comes in an instant... It is the Love-Action of your Brother/Sister-Human.

You saw the world for what it is and know Love Divine for what It is. It was the movement toward Divine Source that has brought about victory over your world. Then you Know, "God, I Am."

~~~~

~Day 23~
Divine Source Guidance

Look for the signs and wonders in your life. They will guide you. If at any time you come to a fork in the road and know not which way to go then open the door to your heart and consider what would be best for all life.

Consider what the creation is... you in your destiny are going toward. Divine Source always knows what is the way to the light. It is always there to give you the answers you need.

If you simply center yourself in the universe and affirm, "I now release my free will and replace it with Love's free will. I know Love is alive and awake, I am too. I am able to see Mother/Father God's perfected love through signs and wonders." It is by God's Grace you are brought into this world, by grace you live in the now and by grace you will ascend into heaven.

Remember to love your family-human and all life. In this bountiful connection you will be given what you need to carry on. There will be peace when you are done.

~~~~

~Day 24~
Holy Healthy & Happy

There are imbalances that exist within your mind that can lead to imperfections in the physical. In correct alignment with universal flow you will always feel holy, happy, and healthy.

Sometimes you need a lesson to show you of the next path to self-development you need to pass down. Be not discouraged by the pitfalls that make your life tough for awhile. Instead, open your eyes even wider and rejoice the Creator.

It is Love, Light and Life, in Its three-fold perfection, that allows you to know if you go off the truest path, for Mother/Father God is constant in Their love and light. You, however, in your not fully developed God-hood must learn through trial and error.

With persistence and a bright love-light you will grow into the holy, happy and healthy perfection of God.

~~~~

Peaceful Coexistence

Come forth Great Brother and Sister and with you bring the light Divine Source has given you that makes us all one. Now is the time and this Sweet Earth is the place. Peaceful coexistence is now ours.

We, throughout the centuries as saint and martyrs, have prayed for it and no invocation to Divine Source is ever unanswered. All goes into its perfect position within the universe and at that very instant becomes a stronghold of peace that can never be destroyed.

Today millions of us are joining as one loving family... We know what we want and by universal principal it is ours. Peace on earth is made reality by the love-nature of Human-Kind.

~~~~

Dress of Love Divine

Into this world you come naked and naked you shall leave. From the moment you are born into carnal flesh you are dressed to the image of human flesh and the disguise of your lower self is all that is perceived.

Depending on the life flow you are moving in you could spend years in this un-enlightened state. Yet, at some point in life you will learn of the dress of Love Divine. Mother/Father God is the light that shines upon everyone who enters into the world.

You must see this light and clothe yourself in it. It is in the pure white garment, symbolized as the God essence within you; you can ascend back to the Mother/Father, not through the path of death, but instead on the path of life upon a shimmering ray from the very heart of God.

Then you will see Human's true purpose.

~~~~

~Day 27~
Let There Be Peace

Let there be peace on earth. Let it flow from the central focus of your being. Forgive and totally release the past. Allow yourself not to harbor feelings of anger, hurt or resentment, for these, however real they may seem to you, are as prison bars. They will hold you tightly to the degree you hold on to them.

Set yourself free. You hold the key to peace. It will be your decision to have peace on earth or to live the hell within.

To gain happiness there is only one choice, love your family-human, all life and especially yourself.

You are the creator of peace on earth. Let it flow into its perfection now!!

~~~~

~Day 28~
You Can Do It

As you love yourself then you will see your journey into Connection with God. Once you come to know yourself you will never have to look outside of yourself to find answers of why your environment is this way or that way, for inside you already know.

It is up to you to find a way to free this wisdom of within. You can do it. It is your destiny to discover your boundless power; your oneness with the universe.

Simply say and know, "I am freeing myself from all negative past experiences. I am one in the Ocean of Living Love. I am in complete charge of my life and love myself fully and unconditionally."

Here, as you realize this with all your heart, mind and strength, you will indeed be free. See yourself and your strength. You will indeed be free. See yourself as the God-Creator you are and in the Forever of the Now you will Fly Free.

~~~~

Everything is Alright

The beloved strength of the Creator pours into your life stream and instantly you feel within you; the flow of light. At last you know everything is alright. Mother Earth is supplying you the power of conception, allowing you to be the creator.

From the ethers a thought form is put out and secured by universal oneness of Love and Truth. It moves to its center nucleus and here the spark of Life is given.

This is the perfect three-fold balance of creation; the Mother of the Earth; the Father of the Heavens and You as a central focus between the two; a divine reaction, the source of all life. In deep adoration your soul sings out in the bliss of Thankfulness.

~~~~

~Day 30~
Actual Peace on Earth

A mission has been bestowed upon us to feed the hungry, free the enslaved and bring light to the multitudes. It is time for the garden to return to the earth. Millions are being asked to carry their burden and travel the often rocky road to peace. They have seen a Vision of Sisterhood and Brotherhood; the Unanimity of the Human Race.

The Glory of victory shines in the yonder land with a brightness that overcomes all evil and obstacles. Truly, the glory of Love is lighting the way.

Perhaps you have seen a glimpse of this new direction of actual peace on earth and desire more. Do not wonder how you can make a difference because just by seeing the light, however small, of the New Age, you are bringing about peace on earth.

The love you bring will free all into a Beautiful River of Life.

~~~~

~Day 31~
Energy Connection

At times in our life we feel full of energy while at other times this nourishment is not with us, consciously. We feel cut off, down and even sometimes depressed.

At these times take extra time to smell the flowers, to give to a loved one or to yourself. It is in these actions the "Energy Connection" is re-established.

Never dwell on how you are not this or that, for you are what you are by what you think you are.

Claim yourself. It is your right to freedom overall. It is by living in the light all things are attainable. Arise now and take charge of you life.

~~~~

~Day 32~
Mission Know Self

Everybody is sent into this world with a mission. It is a mission to know ones self to such a deep level you know Mother/Father God.

No lesson is ever given without a test. You may say to yourself, "At last, I have achieved Freedom." Divine Source will test your integrity and, by the degree of your faith, bring you exactly what you need to enslave or to truly free you.

The choice is always yours. Fear not the test, expect them and accept them with all your heart, soul, mind and strength. It is always by this acceptance, to the best of your ability; You are set Free.

~~~~

~Day 33~
Dreams Made Reality

Have you ever come to a point in your life when you did not understand something? You question, saying "What's this or that supposed to mean?" Yet, even in your confusion, you knew what ever it was; it was good.

Keep in mind that those who believe, without actually knowing, are doubly blessed, for it is easy to believe something we can see. With faith, however, the impossible can be accomplished. A dream can be made reality with the correct amount of faith, sparked by action.

So the next time you see the light at the end of the tunnel; follow that light no matter how many miles you must tread. The answer will come to you by focusing at the end of your journey, where the beacon originates.

Though at times the light may seem to falter and disappear; keep the Faith of its brilliance and you'll be led to Heaven's Gate.

~~~~

~Day 34~
Selfless Service

In living a life of selfless service you can learn to find yourself and your power to give and receive. Place yourself in the involvement of what needs to be done. If you see it as a free gift of the universe that has brought you to this point of service you will go far in receiving bountifully for the gift you give.

Detach yourself from the consequence of what this will bring you... Set it free and it will bless you, for you came into this world with nothing. All you have has been given to you from the resources of Love Divine. Is it not time for you to give back to Universal Source as freely as It has given to you?

This is the way to receive the bounties of life. Place no limit on the world and no limit will be placed on you.

~~~~

~Day 35~
Special Gift

To be kind and share of yourself is a special gift. To give a light to a sister or brother who stumbles in the dark will your soul begin to lift.

You have something special in you you can choose to use; it is a heart. You can choose to keep it trapped inside or to bring together that which is apart.

See yourself as a real giver to all life. This alone will take you through all strife.

Feel at ease in this and do as you please. The heaven on earth will come to you as a simple ease.

Within you is the power to give so much. With your love-nature it will be as the golden touch.

A beautiful thing will happen this day. This is given to you that you may have true happiness, I pray.

~~~~

Accept the Love

When a love comes into your life do not fight it; saying within, "I am not worthy of this beauty." Nothing is ever sent to you by accident. All you have earned.

Go with the motion the universe has supplied you. Acting as a center of this relationship many great lessons can be learned. Just allow yourself to accept the love offered freely with open heart and open arms.

The victory of wisdom awaits you if you approach all experiences in this manner. The circle of Love or fear; as you give you shall receive.

In your heart flows a mighty river. Let it fill the very essence of your world. You truly deserve all the love you give. Accept it Now.

~~~~

~Day 37~
Aquarian Age Peace

The New Age is here. The time of the game of war and the pain of hunger are removed forever. It has not been an easy climb, many have fell by the way-side, only to be picked up and even sometimes carried to those lofty heights. We have seen the world transform from the shadows of darkness into the ecstasy of Light Supreme.

Many of us knew it was coming. This was the signpost to the reality we have created... The glorious peace on Earth of the Aquarian Age.

Give thanks to the one and all for this noble deed. Now we bow before the One Creator and by our magnified Love-Light we instill gratitude for the greatest of all; The Gift of Life Everlasting.

~~~~

~Day 38~
Choose God-Light

Bring your mind to center focus. Let this focus be a way of peace; a way brotherhood and to an actual garden on Earth. It is in reality this central focus of being will bring about the Change!!

You hold the very key within your hand and the door way is through the passage of the heart. So stand tall, my beloved. Know if you will but choose to be a channel of the pure God-Light then all this will go beyond the simple words written here. They will manifest into the divine goal of all life; Peace with yourself and flowing oneness with the Creator.

Choose now in the victory of Love and so it is.

~~~~

~Day 39~
Universe in Action

Have you ever made a promise to somebody and knew it so deep in your heart that it became a promise to Universal Divine Source? If you have then, perhaps, you have seen the actual workings of the universe in action. You've experienced the connections of the finite self with the infinite self.

This is why, as you really believed in your heart, you could accomplish your goal, for the universe loves a lover and responds in miraculous ways to return what you put into it. This is why many Masters (you are a master too) were given all power in heaven and earth.

They knew of their connectedness with universal source. They allowed their being to totally merge with it. The resources of the universe are yours if you become One with All.

~~~~

~Day 40~
You're the Master

Free yourself, my brother, my sister... as I look inside. Stop saying, "I think I can" or "Maybe if." You hold the key to your destiny, nobody else has that right or honor.

If you are sad and confused and know not which way to go, don't wallow in it and listen to yourself say, "I'm stuck. I don't know where to go." These are very powerful affirmations; in a negative since. As you have so decreed, so will it be done.

Stop it!! Take control of your life. You are the master. Affirm to yourself, "Yes, I can do whatever I can imagine." Never say, "Never." In Divine Source's way all things are attainable. Be strong, my child, and stand firm with your convictions.

Peace of Mind can be yours.

~~~~

~Day 41~
Receiver Lights Glow

The Joy of Sharing. The Beauty of Giving. These are special gifts from God. If at any time you are feeling down and really can't put your finger on the reason why; turn it around. Don't use that energy to follow the pattern of the blues.

You can make something really great out of it. As it is given from your heart (not out of guilt or obligation) you will see the light within the receiver start to glow. This wondrous light will soon brighten you and instead of the shadows you will see the spirit of happiness come over you.

Always remember; You are the best friend you will ever have... So give to someone who is really special. It is in giving to yourself that your love nature will open up to boundless splendor, for as you love yourself you will find it easy to love everything else. Then Mother/Father God will smile on you with the beautiful riches of Heaven.

~~~~

~Day 42~
Passing of Time

The years that go by taking us along with them. We see them come and we see them go. It, in its movement, gives many people many different reflections. Some of us are sad, while others are glad.

It is your choice what you make of the years as they flow by. A million things can be accomplished or only a few. On the spiritual path you will be lead into a space where time is irrelevant.

It may seem at times few events are taking place; but know they are the ones that are right for you here and now. These few, once on the true path, have the power of millions of happenings.

So be not concerned with the passing of time. In Love Divine you will do just what you need to do. Just relax and flow with it and you will see.

~~~~

~Day 43~
Beyond Physicality

The purpose of our lives is to free ourselves from all barriers that keep us from experiencing Love Divine to the fullest.

We can see the effects of Mother/Father God by the love, light and life we experience; yet, we can not hold these physically in our hand. This tells us that all things in this world that can be held and touched are not, by themselves, what is important.

It is the holding onto the physicality of them you entrap yourself. When you move beyond, into the love, light and life, you then see the inner beauty. As you are truly there then nothing can stop you from being a part, a whole, of the Creator-God.

Drop attachments you have to the physical and you will be Happy and Free.

~~~~

~Day 44~
Rocky Roads

In this life we experience many rocky roads. Some of these we choose directly, while others might appear to be forced upon us. Let us consider the ones chosen.

In reality, all roads are our choice. Somewhere, somehow in this lifetime or past lifetimes our thoughts, words or actions have generated the experiences of today. Rocky they may be; the choice will and has always been ours.

To work your way through any incorrect decisions you have made in the past you can sit back and let them eventually circle back to you or you can live a life of service, gratitude and sacrifice. Choosing the harder path will perhaps lead you into victory; for Divine Source loves a giver.

The choice is yours; rocky or smooth, now or later!

~~~~

~Day 45~
Cosmic Spark Reunited

It is said that we all originated from the spark of the Mother-Father God. A single spark from the heart of God; divided equally into... Female and Male.

Then we are made manifest on this world of form and third dimension. We two, male and female, are separated. It is our destiny to reunite this cosmic spark. It keeps us moving on from lifetime to lifetime; from relationship to relationship seeking the true oneness with our mate.

In our searching we create or work through much karma. As we come closer to our Divine Creator, in all we do, so do we come closer to our original spark alive in another person.

Keep searching with all the love you have and you will once again join with the perfect One of Mother-Father God.

~~~~

Guiding Light

Into this world I have been sent to be a guiding light to all. Where the hungry is, then so shall I be with the Bread of Life. Where there is disease then also I'll be there with the loving, healing hand of Mother/Father God.

The purpose of my life is to fling open the prison bars of the hearts of all mankind, for I am light; the light and love that overcomes all darkness in this world. You need only believe in the Divine Presence; the connection allowing you to flow for the magnificent development of the Divinity in Humankind.

You are me and I am you, as we move into this greater reality. See and know from your heart-center, "I am the Master."

~~~~

~Day 47~
Come Together

Within all life there is a natural tendency to come together, to unify and become one. It is in this drawing together that strength is made manifest. Think of it as a law of the universe.

In the conception that time is eternal we can see that everything must create (unifying) to maintain this eternalness. If a single thing ever destroyed itself and truly became nothing (instead of evolving) then by this very action over a period of eons of time the universe would become nothing.

Nothingness is an impossibility. This is why power is found in the creative touching together of life. It is the power of Love Divine that sustains all life.

With the art of creativeness the secrets of the universe are realized.

~~~~

~Day 48~
Time and Space Flow

Certain days can be very special, especially when you put forth into the ethers that this day will be special. All of the universe and its connections of time seem to come to you when you, from deep within, believe this is a special day.

Life is such a wondrous thing when you begin to realize connectedness... From this focus you are happy and living without doubt. This allows you to flow in the rhythm of time and space.

Wake up each day and know, "Today is a Special Day." Sure enough, it will be... God in action and you in God. A flowing of each day into the perfection you may have before only imagined. Now, by will, it is Reality.

~~~~

~Day 49~
Your Destiny

In life there are many temptations that can lead you down this path and that path. In dealing with these it is necessary to see what your destiny is.

True, there may be many ways to get there, but by learning the lessons of the way you choose you save much time. Many people, for awhile, end up on the path of loop after loop. They simply are blind to what they need to see, learn and know.

Rise above this, my friend. Become familiar with universal law... for it is a combination of you and it that determines if you will reach your destiny now or in many lifetimes.

Be at peace with yourself and flow as a mighty river of Love... You will rise above it all.

~~~~

~Day 50~
Your Home-Land

Within the focus of the heart of Divine Source you can live free. You can fly up to the peaks of life (no matter how high) and rest in perfect contentment.

The beauties of the Eternal Garden awaits you. They call for you and bring you ever onward to your home-land. All this is by being a centered being and loving all life. Imagine this and crystallize it into perfect manifestation.

You need only to affirm it is so and it will be; by Love's Grace. These are not just simple nice words you can read and not see results. They are reality and as you live them to the fullest love you have, then you will be enlightened by the presence of Mother/Father God.

~~~~

~Day 51~
Stand Fast in Light

In light we can all stand if we would only take a stand. It is up to us to bring about understanding if a situation is shrouded in confusion. It is in this stand the answers will begin to flow.

At first the flow may seem slow but if you are determined and stand fast, without weakness or doubt, then the universe will rush to your assistance. The wisdom you need to know will be supplied.

In other words, there is no such thing as darkness or not knowing. There is Always a way if you stand firm in your convictions and faith. The truth of the matter is that you already know the answers.

Stand forth in full power and dominion and it will be yours.

~~~~

~Day 52~
Full Dominion

Peace be with you, my child. You are the creator and make your own happiness. Bring forth your own light and fly free with the law of Mother/Father God. This is the law of love and truth.

Yes, you can climb any mountain and swim any sea if you would only will to... completely free of doubt and fear.

A dream of millions in these early days of the Aquarian Age is Peace, an actual Garden on earth. This is and will happen. "How?" you may ask... Simply by people standing forth in full dominion, in flow with God and saying, " It is done and it is so. I Am."

~~~~

~Day 53~
Illumined I Move Freely

I have been down the golden trail on the way of the evolution of my soul and the soul of all life. I have tasted the sweetness of the nectar of Love Divine.

From the very center of my heart I sing praises and bow with my all to the Creator, for now I know we are one. Love has shown me a light and illumined I move freely down the path of my true destiny on this earth.

Thank you my brothers and sisters for the "I Am" of who you are. You take away all darkness and awaken me to the highest realization. Peace is ours if we only but love.

~~~~

~Day 54~
Love and Light

Yes, as I will it, the light pours into me and I see the connection between the light I am and the love Divine Source is. In realization, I see there is no difference between love and light, for they are one and the same.

As you love you no longer operate in darkness; You are en-light-ened to true God Reality. When you see the truth and the shadows of illusion disappear there are no barriers to stand in your way. Your love nature illumines the way.

This is the love/light connection, as you will it, extending your heart out to all life, then the light will be there. All things are attainable. You need only to love.

~~~~

~Day 55~
Illuminated Heart Flame

I know within me there burns a great light to illumine my way down paths of darkness and confusion. I know this light is brilliant, in line with the light and love of Mother/Father God.

All I need to do is will it, affirming, "God's will be done" and this mighty flood will burst out from my heart center. All near this illuminated heart flame will feel the essence of the Love nature of God. They will feel good.

Yes, a great power rest within me, wanting to be released to fly gently into the hearts of others. Will I free it? Will I do the will of Love Divine? Yes, I will! I am One!

~~~~

~Day 56~
Divine Love's Time

In this life if we learn to practice patience then all things can be ours. We should never let go of our goals in sight, yet instead, keep them perfectly focused in our mind and heart. Say and know, "It will be done in Divine Love's time, not mine."

There is an all pervasive power that controls the manifestation of your dreams and desires. Grasp it and know it IS alive and in action. Your faith in this true connection will show you to the light as you will it.

All journeys in life show their path. We are the one who must take the first step, followed by another. Peace will be ours as we step and work in the divine order of Love and Truth.

~~~~

~Day 57~
Truth Sets You Free

I fly as a mighty eagle as I tell, see and do the truth in all aspects of my life, for just as Divine Source is love, It is also truth.

Love Divine never goes against Its nature. It is always in perfect alignment. Its will is perfect. This, too, I must be, as must all humans if they are to truly be one with Mother/Father God.

Yes, the truth will set you free. If it is working in perfect order in your life you will not be blocked by misconceptions and pseudo reality. You will be free.

You say you do not always know what is true. Love to your very best ability in all ways and the truth will reveal itself.

~~~~

~Day 58~
The True Smile

The magnificence of the New Age is dawning upon us. The Power of Love is overpowering the love of power. Though many say, "Look at the terrible shape the world is in." They see only man's injustice to man. They see only what they want to see.

In truth, all humans, both individually and collectively, have the love essence within them. They know when they are truly smiling and of the true smile of others. This smile is formed in the happiness of love.

The smiles are increasing and with them the mountain of true peace is starting to shine forth. It is happening! Open your eyes and you will see.

~~~~

~Day 59~
The Way to Peace

May the peace that is Love Divine be in your heart. Love will bless you if you rise up right now and sing Its praise. Go forward into the world of strife and sorrow and know that your true power is found with your faith in Mother/Father God.

Yes, this is the way to peace. The wings of this freedom are composed of pure light. They light your way when the mystery surrounds you. You have learned the path and now fly freely into the very heart of God.

Love, yes love, has shown you to what is right. Do not fear, go powerfully forth. All things are attainable for you, my beloved child, have found the key to Divine Source and love all unconditionally.

~~~~

~Day 60~
The Light

Within all there is contained a light. The light that illumines all is the very light that you see within your mind as you dream.

This light is the divine light of God. It is Love's being in Action. At times you say, "I've seen the light." What you mean by this is that you have come to an understanding.

No longer is it shrouded in darkness or confusion. It has come to the light. This is the light of consciousness, the very same light found in all life.

Come to recognize light as divine intelligence, for indeed, it is the guidance that leads us to all comprehension. Mother/Father God is light. In Them there is no darkness at all. Be Light!!

~~~~

~Day 61~
River of Love

Within all there is a flowing River of Love. It is the most powerful river in the universe. It is the most gentle; flowing ever gently in its caressing manner bringing life to all it touches. It touches all. It brings life to all.

The universe is literally teeming with life from this wonderful river of love. Divine Source so loved the world It brought forth the sustainer as an example of Its love. When we live in the path of the sustainer, focused in love and truth, we rise up our mortal being and become one with the Great Eternal One.

Love and Light and Life in perfect accord in heaven on earth.

~~~~

~Day 62~
I Love You

In the name of truth and love I rise up to the very heart of Mother/Father God this day and with all my being I say unto you, "I Love You." I know that heaven is right here on earth as I extend the love in my heart center out to the heart centers of all life.

Together and as one, you now fly into the grandest splendor of Light Supreme. What a gift it is to share with all creation this gift of life.

"Peace! Peace on earth and Goodwill to all." The Master has spoken these words and wants you to engulf your soul in the spirit of Happiness. At last we have found the way. It is through the action of Love.

~~~~

~Day 63~
Love's Divine Charge

If you want to accomplish your goal in life you must set your spiritual eyes on it and imagine it with the full power of your concentration. Then release it, saying and knowing, "Not my will be done, but Love's."

Divine Source will bring about the manifestation of the goal as your focus is aligned with It. This means you do not simply sit back and wait for it to happen. You must take charge of your life, putting forth the very strength that makes you a divine person. This is being in alignment with Love's Divine Will.

The end result, as the oneness is realized, is now your goal will be seen with your physical eyes. Thank God.

~~~~

The Pledge

I make a pledge to myself this day. This is a pledge to my higher self, for I recognize this as being a part of all higher selves and an underlying principle of the universe.

To this mighty source I say, "I Love You." I will fearlessly go forth and recognize your light and give it in abundance to the People of the World. I will move forward mightily in love.

More and more I will accomplish in giving light to all life. I am joyfully dancing and singing the Divine news and with it I wield my sword of truth. All illusion is cut lose.

I am all powerful. The Divine One is with me. I shall not fear.

~~~~

~Day 65~
Life Anew

Today I begin my life anew. Whatever I wish to accomplish today I will, for today the fear that once ruled my life has been replaced by love.

With this love all walls I see will crumble and my inner fortitude of love and truth will march on. It joins with the "righteous" ones of all mankind and is instantly as powerful as Universal Source.

In this new life only forward steps are taken. They will know of my love by my example. They will know of the Divine Soul by seeing it manifest in their personal lives as they go forth in Divine Love.

All will work out because we only do the will of Universal Source. We receive this Love.

~~~~

~Day 66~
Peace On Earth

If you truly want peace on earth then you must think, talk and act in a peaceful manner. The world is a reflection of what you are. It is the fear you possess and it is the love you possess. Why not love and see this love manifest on a world level?

Only peace comes through peace. In truth, the pure light within is a beacon for all to follow. Know this and shine forth this inner light to all life.

You are the creator and make reality what it is. Be peace and peace will surely be. Free yourself of self-limitations and become all powerful, one with Universal Divine Source.

Peace awaits the journeyer and their victory will be true happiness.

~~~~

~Day 67~
Universal Bounties

Today I will accomplish a multitude of goals. All in my life is coming together as I will it to be.

Today I will smile at the world and all who see this smile will be lifted up. I am a child of the universe and know that today, as I put forth my very best, the universe and all Its bounties will be mine.

The direction is clear, the writing is upon the walls. I will follow my heart and it will give me strength to accomplish my goals of the short and long term.

Yes, Universal Source does listen and responds. Now it is up to the mighty and loving to carry the load to success.

~~~~

Small Still Voice

When one listens to the small, still voice within they are in reality in tune with the Omnipotent, the universal mind. This presence is all-knowing, all-loving and all-powerful.

It is no wonder the truly faithful "Small" have such great strength in this perilous world around us. Within they listen and hear. They know Divine Source, The Comforter, is always there.

It is ever so gentle this voice, yet remember true love always gives you ultimate freewill. Become one with this spirit of beauty and you will hear and know the great universal secret... All is Light. There is no darkness at all.

~~~~

~Day 69~
Universal Source is Real

With all the love in my heart I look into your eyes, the windows to your soul, and say to you, "Divine Universal Source is Real." The universal mind, that connects us all into one, is proof of the existence of Its being.

The rainbow is the writing upon the walls of consciousness. It is the foundation stone upon which rests the Great Eternal Living Truth and the Love of all creation.

The truth will set you free. Accept this truth of Divine Universality and no longer will you stumble in darkness, for All is Light. Feel at peace in the loving arms of the Creator.

Eternal life awaits you as you believe, know and act. Peace be with you my child.

~~~~

~Day 70~
Keep Up

To Keep Up in life is one of the greatest gifts. It is through this added measure of effort the mountain that appears in your dreams and desires will seem small and its summit just a matter of always putting one step in front of the last.

Keep up no matter the obstacles, smile at the hardships, laugh at the pain and feel joyful when yet another rock appears in your way.

By Keeping up the battle with the "tormentor" will only be the battle within. With faith and persistence you can say, "Be you mountain removed," and it will.

Keep Up, my love, and all will flow in perfect harmony and the Grace of Universal Presence will guide you to victory!

~~~~

~Day 71~
Divine's Crystal Ball

Come and look into my crystal ball and you will see visions of Grandeur of a world to come. Not the sob story some would lead you to believe, but one of victory and success for all of mankind, indeed all life.

The hungry, homeless and tempest tossed will feel the love coming from the hearts of humanity and feel the freedom only the Masters now enjoy.

The Garden will be on earth and the abundance of Universal Divine Source will flow as a mighty river bringing life anew and a sweet healing to the nations.

Love will prove its glorious connection as its abounding power brings Joy to the Seekers of Peace.

~~~~

Rainbow of Love

There is a Divine and Omnipotent communication to be made with the Rainbow. Its beauty radiates down from above from the very face of the Creator. With love and gratitude it is sent down from the heavens as a gift of peace to Earth's children.

As Divine Source is the creator, so are we the co-creator. With our love we can make this communication of Love, the rainbow, a true sign of the Beauty of Life.

It is our living fountain of healing waters made manifest as we follow its example of unity; "One for all, All for one.

Truly the love of Divine Source has sent it and truly the love of humanity will be set Free through its grace and beauty.

~~~~

~Day 73~
Commitment to Grow

As one commits their self to a goal, project or dream they have already accomplished the greatest part of this task. It is in the commitment we grow to understand, through practice, the way we can manifest this desire.

The commitment keeps us ever stepping forward. Rocks, valleys and mountains may lay I our way but within our heart of hearts we have said we would continue toward our goal, "No matter what."

We grow to love what lies beyond those distant barriers. We send out a light within that, from the very start, illumines what we are destined to achieve. Yet, we must commit and do what we know is right to achieve the mighty plan. It all works in perfect order. Will You??

~~~~

~Day 74~
Creation's Wonder

Glory be to Divine Source and the glories of Creation for it has been to brought to light that through this light we may be conscious of the wonders of nature. It is all so beautiful.

What a gift these flowers and trees and birds are... All in perfect order with the millions of other facets of the Creator's work. What a marvel it is that we, too, have had our hand in this creation. It came from Divine Source and became manifest as we became conscious of it.

The beauty you see, it came from the beauty of Human. All things that are wonderful came about because We are wonderful. Be not fooled by the skeptics for you are the Creator. You have the power to Love.

~~~~

~Day 75~
Our Shared Light

You light up my life. When I am with you our lights come together and become as one. The light we share is the light all human beings, indeed all life, share. It is the light of Divine Source.

You, as you move into my heart flame, bring an added measure of Love to my life. Oh, the glory of it, to feel your love while you share my love. Our love lights the earth.

When you come forth in mighty power, yet with the peace of a daisy in the summer rain, I feel this peace and I am nourished by its awesome beauty and power.

We have now joined one with the nature of Divine Source. Thank you for your light, love and peace. Your grace gives me hope.

~~~~

Creation's Song

Is it not so that all of creation sings forth with the wonder of their creative expression? I, too, if I am to be one with nature, can and must sing forth with an expression of beauty of the Creator's work.

When I put forth that beauty I am on equal ground with the beauty of nature. Therefore, I will see the beauty in all that surrounds me, never focusing on the shadows. I set myself free.

The wind, being one with natural flow, will guide me to the perfect place to go. Always will I express the beauty for I am certainly meant to be here now.

All will come to see the beauty and feel the love of my being.

~~~~

Today's Love Step

What a special day today is, for today is the first day of the rest of my life. I can choose victory this day or I can choose defeat. It all lies ahead in the pathway to the right or left.

I can only put one foot in front of the other and say, "Love's will be done." Its glory will guide me down the path which is best.

Today I make my own happiness. I choose to be happy and with the glowing essence of my being brighten the day of others. I choose today to love everybody unconditionally, for all have a lesson for me.

Today is a perfect day to love and be loved, for today I live in the Divine Light.

~~~~

Home Divine

Let there be light on the earth to guide the weary home. Let there be love in this home that they may feel the glowing essence of Source's being. Let life always flourish in abundance on this earth, flowing into the one perfect soul.

Grace be with you my child and share it. Together, you and me, one with the Creator, we can live in love and light. It brightens the way to come and see.

They will see harmony and as they raise their voices in song they will glow to warm the earth even more. It is all so beautiful to see us join as one with Divine Essence, the Creator.

We can now co-create the universe and know of the Garden of Eternal Life.

~~~~

~Day 79~
Steering to Freedom

Within your hands is a steering wheel. This can steer you to wherever you want to go in life.

You, in your actions, can bind yourself and cause the universal flow to slow and restrict your ultimate turning ability. You must operate with and for universal principle, do so in the spirit of Love and Truth.

The truth is; you are a very powerful being, able to conquer ALL strife as you come forth in Love. Go forward, always saying, "Yes I Can and I Am."

The key is in your belief in your divine power and loving all strife free. Steer it to its supreme destiny and set yourself free.

~~~~

~Day 80~
Bridge to the Heavens

May the joy, which is love, be with you. Go forward in full dominion as a beacon of the heart. Smile on the situations that confront you and know you are victorious as you bring forth a sword of truth and the bridge of love.

Be pure of heart, soul and mind and be proud of who you are, for you are the gift of the pure Love's essence as you come forth in harmony with Divine Source's being.

Above all, my child, Love; for this is the bridge to the heavens... From love of all life you will always be in the grace of creative flow.

Divine Source has a special plan for you. Will you charge forth as the great living being you are and show many the light? Say, "I Am."

~~~~

A Matter of Belief

What a victory we live in when we say, "Yes I can," and then in faith supreme go forth and accomplish that mighty task.

It is all a matter of belief and then taking those fearless steps forward, standing tall internally and externally no matter what comes your way. It is a matter of loving it Free.

Whether it is small or large it must be set free with our unconditional love, for when we fear, saying, "Maybe or we'll see," then we hold our goal captive and not able to do its divine work.

Victory is always found in complete love. Know you can and you will. The blessed assurance of the Masters rests with you for They know all things are possible if you Fly Free and fear not.

~~~~

Faith gives grace

You ~~are~~ Matter

~Day 82~
Divine Flow

The love only the Masters have experienced is now starting to manifest on the earth plane. We have found a way to open our hearts and minds to Divine Flow. We are letting the creative flow be the light that is illuminating from all of life.

Great joy of victory is rising up as we lift our voices in song. In harmony we carry The Word of Spiritual Freedom to the oppressed and they are set free. Peace now flows as a mighty river restoring all life back into the perfection and loving arms of Divine Source.

All is in perfect order. We bow as one before this divine light and know it was all by Divine and Loving Grace.

~~~~

~Day 83~
Freely Give

"Freely you have received, freely give." What marvelous words these are for within their message is the open doorway to all success, happiness and Universal Abundance.

Truly the universe flows with the eternal fountain of life. This brings forth all our dreams and desires, in accord with the will of Divine Source. Of course, we never really own anything accept our individuality. We must not attach ourselves to anything.

Free it all since it is all a free gift anyway. When you do the rivers of abundance will flow your way. In your free gift you will find a place in the heart of Love Divine.

~~~~

~Day 84~
Find the Neutral Position

We may have many ups and downs in this life of ours on hourly, daily and even yearly levels. Even minute by minute we can lose our central focus and be tossed into an emotional high or low.

If we are to be happy, most of the time, we must find the neutral position and revel in it. All actions have an equal and reflective reaction. It is for this reason we find ourselves on the see-saw of life if we over elate or over depress ourselves.

Find your center and therein you will find Divine Source for It works from all centers. Herein you can rest peacefully. The balance between up and down is maintained.

Be neutral and move forward and you will be happy most of the time.

~~~~

~Day 85~
Choose to Live It

What a miracle life could be if we would only choose to live it. So many directions, so many wonders are ours to have. It is all truly a gift from Divine Source, It being here to keep us happy and keep us ever striving for what is best.

Accept this miracle of life and with humble gratitude give thanks to Mother/Father God. Showing you are humble and a servant of the creative function, all power in heaven and earth will be yours.

What a miracle to be able to give and receive the bounties of the Universal Presence. Now is the time to accept and live in accord with divine principle. In truth, We are Kings and Queens as we love.

~~~~

~Day 86~
Behold Yourself

Come forth Oh Great Children of wonder and know that the Masters walk with you. Feel Their presence as you go out into the world and know you can make a difference, for these Ones are not only outside they are also within you.

Behold Yourself!! You are the master of your reality as you take charge of your life. Feel at peace. Your soul has become one with the One Great Soul.

It all works together as one, giving you perfect guidance down your path to unfold. Yes, the Masters are alive and working wonders in your life. Accept you and they are one and love will always light your way.

~~~~

~Day 87~
I Am the Victor

We, today, are moving into a day we have never before ventured into. A day, as it is our will, that can hold the miracle of whatever we desire it to be.

The choice is always ours. Will the choice be for success or failure? The internal projection we hold will bring us either one, for we can choose to love or to fear; to be with the universal flow or against it.

By saying, "I am the victor and now take charge of my life," you do. Our light of love becomes manifest. Believe in yourself for today is the most important day of your life.

Live in the essence of Mother/Father God and succeed.

~~~~

~Day 88~
With Wings Take Flight

You are the perfection of nature made manifest. You are the gift you bring to all life and the ability to behold this creation in your mind and heart.

See yourself as free as a bird; coming, going and flowing with the passing wind. With wings you take flight into the New Beginning. Feel your power. Feel the purity and strength of a mighty white horse.

Become one with these aspects of creation and see it as you; purely powerful and flying free with wings of silver. Grace and freedom is yours as you visualize yourself as part and one with the many creations the marvel of nature offers. Love and Hope abound.

~~~~

~Day 89~
Spread the Joy

Laugh and the world will laugh with you, cry and the world will do the same. Is it not better to spread the joy and the happiness instead of the sorrow? Is there not a direction your soul knows it must go? Then laugh and spread the joy found with God's will.

You are the creator and do make a difference to all the life-streams around you. You can and will be great happiness and victory to people as you reach out in the image of Mother/Father God.

Feel good that you rest in the hands of Divine Source. Receive Its Power and give to the people of the nations of the world. Your laugh will make all the difference.

~~~~

Divine Love's Will

To love somebody unconditionally means that you accept them the way they are. You place no limitations on the path they are on, for they have chosen it, for them it may be the quickest way to Divine Source.

It is a way to have them see what is right and what is wrong. Let them be their own guide. Let God be the guiding source in their lives. If you want change in their lives then say, "Divine Love's will be done, not mine."

Love them, above all love them, for Divine Source is Love. It is all of our destinies to work our way back to the Creator. With faith and hope and knowing it will all work out in perfect accord if you love.

~~~~

~Day 91~
Heights of Exultation

If, in my life, I could rise above my fears and limitations I could soar as a mighty eagle to heights of exultation. The love in my heart, which to this point I have mostly just talked about, would find a myriad places to associate itself with.

It will no longer be trapped by the illusion of pain and separateness. It will fly forth in victory and the one unifying light. Grace will guide it along its way into the perfect unfoldment.

Fear and illusions is all that is stopping this love from doing its mighty work. Taking control of my life I say, "I am successful. I fear not and fly freely into bold new realities."

~~~~

~Day 92~
Pass with Love

If I shall pass this earthly plane before my journey is through, let me pass as one who has shown love and has nourished by it. Let them see the truth I have extended from every part of my being.

Let them feel the grace I have channeled as I became one with Divine Source, Loving them and all life unconditionally. All will be in perfect accord when that day comes for I will live in the light today and always strive to do what is right.

A smile and the hand of my love and of the Greater Self I bring to all. They will come to know me as a Child of God, in truth.

~~~~

~Day 93~
Peace Abounding

What a pleasure it is to salute the one in all in the land of wonder and awe, for now peace is abounding on earth. The strength of the Divine and Holy Self has made manifest this wonderful way of life.

Everywhere one looks they see beauty and a grace of togetherness among all life. We have brought our minds to a single focus and this focus brings us to the light.

We are now the light of the world. Great thanksgiving resounds from the heart of every man, woman and child. We sing Divine Love's praises and receive eternal life.

We bow to the creative center flying free in the Garden that is now earth.

~~~~

~Day 94~
Sing of Divine Source

As my daily devotion I will sing of Divine Source. With a song in my heart I will go about my day and be in harmony with the world around me.

Everywhere I go people will see a light exuding from me. They will come to know this light as love, peace, tranquility, happiness and goodwill.

They will share in my being and be lifted by it. Together we will fly and be still in Love's will. All situations in our lives will float gently into our life-streams and be handled with Grace Supreme.

The song of the love of life will be the key. Hand and heart we accept it today.

~~~~

~Day 95~
Stand Up

There comes a time in everybody's life they must stand up on their feet and with heart-felt integrity do what is right. They must ask for the light of love to guide their decisions and always come from a perspective of unconditional love and oneness.

If this means the moving away from the physical life-stream of someone or something then So Be It! Send forth Pure Love Essence to this person or situation and let divine will take its play.

It will all work out in perfect order as you are in the light of love and what is good, holy and just. Divine Source helps us if we can not find strength within.

May Divine Love's will be done.

~~~~

~Day 96~
Infinite Well of Love

Deep at the center of my being there is an infinite well of love. Will I take charge of my life and allow this mighty source to flow forth? Will I share it with many and all to nourish the weak and hungry?

Yes, and forever yes, this is my will for it is the will of Mother/Father God. Divine Source gives love in an infinite amount of ways. Its love is the river and the giver of life. I am a part of this river. How could I flow against its loving touch?

All I have to do is say, "I Am." I am one with Divine Source and flow ever perfectly with the Divine River of Life. I now accept this is done, as Love's most Holy Name, "I Am."

~~~~

~Day 97~
A Perfect Mate

Within this world is a perfect mate for all people. Each of us come from the one Godhead and split into a dual spark. We go our separate ways on the earth plane.

One day our return to our creative source will bring us back together as one. We will be united in love and truth, which is God. With flowing beauty and grace we have said, "Love's will be done," and it is.

We now embrace, as the dew on the early morning violet caresses the gift of life. All is in perfect divine order and our strength, now again as one, carries the light of love high.

Peace is in our hearts and we are home.

~~~~

~Day 98~
The Comforter

Through the valley of discouragement we may walk, yet say and know in our heart, "I will fear no evil, for love is with me."

Ever I will move forward and see what is behind the mystery that enshrouds my vision. Great is the one who gives all, doing so because the "Comforter" is showing the way.

I Am fearless and one with God, who is Love. With a mighty roar all know this fearless one is coming whose presence lights hearts and minds with the brightness of the sun.

Great victory is found for those who love and fear not. Take hold of this mighty truth and the grace of Divine Source will be with you.

~~~~

~Day 99~
Best in All Situations

In this world there are many ways to toil and labor, many ways to be tested, ever testing our endurance, strength and patience.

From this moment on I accept the path given to me. I will see it as a mighty gift and from it I will squeeze the fruit of success. I will taste the sweetness of life.

Always will I see the best in all situations, never will I let discouragement or the bitterness dim my vision. Only great victory is mine. All else is less than the Godhead.

I will take the fruits of life and brighten every moment of every single day. The seed of this fruit will bring about a garden in my heart and others will rejoice in Garden Paradise.

~~~~

~Day 100~
One with Love

The ability to achieve anything in the world is at my feet. All that needs to be said is, "Love's will be done" and "I am one with Love."

With this magical combination the grace of the Divine and Holy will be with me. In fact, as I put forth the full power of Love Supreme, in truth, I will be the Master of my reality.

Living within the nature of God all things are possible. Victory awaits at the turn of the road. I will salute the one in all for this great life is what gives beauty to the flowers and all of creation.

One need only open their eyes and the radiant beauty will shine in their lives and they will be born anew.

~~~~

~Day 101~
Sweet Taste Ahead

Keeping my heart and mind tuned in on the sweet taste ahead, I rejoice in the will of Divine Source, for I know things are looking up for the Human Family.

We are beginning to take wings and the clause, "One for all and all for one," is taking on its highest
contextual meaning. We are truly becoming one with Mother/Father God and They are becoming one with us.

Great hymns of Thanksgiving spring forth and smiles are beginning to glow as never before. What a glorious day. Together singing the tune of love in truth as the abundance of the world's resources are given ever freely from the heart. How sweet it is.

~~~~

~Day 102~
Smile in My Heart

With a smile in my heart I will greet this day. I will lovingly greet each situation, for I know as I smile the Soul of my being smiles with me.

In truth, I will not see the pain and the anguish that is around me and even share in at times, for these are of the lower consciousness and will pass away before the dew touches another Spring morning.

In the grace of Divine promise I shall remain, for I am reminded, "Always remember, I am always with you." God is love, the fountain of life eternal bringing light to the illusion of these so-called emotions.

In Divine Heart is where I want to be. The light of love flourishes and peace, sweet peace, is found.

~~~~

~Day 103~
Faith Removes Mountains

Knock and the door shall be opened for you. Ask and you shall receive. Give and it shall be given unto you.

What mighty words of truth these are, for we are the Creators. If we move into our heart center and within desire a change, it will be given to us. Peace of mind awaits us as we move forward from this point of knowing.

It is faith that removes mountains and helps us cross the valleys of life. It is the power within, in tune with the creative flow, that brings forth the abundance on earth as it is in heaven.

Use it, believe it, become one with it and always reach out in loving and growing ways, for you are the creator and make your own happiness.

~~~~

Think Positive

It is like a motto for the New Age, "Keep Up and Think Positive." No longer do we need to dwell in compromise or defeat, we have came, saw and conquered. We now live in Harmony with the Soul of our being, the true King within all.

We bow before the alter found at the center of our heart and instantly become of service to the One in All. The reflection of this shines from all points of the universe and truly all power in heaven and earth is ours.

With great blessings I now go forth as a Chalice of God's Will. I am light, love and life. What great victories are ours as we Keep Up, Keep Positive and smile with the grace of living loving light.

~~~~

Dance at Center

Sometimes in our lives we have to grab the bull by the horns and face ourselves in the greatest challenge of our lives. We have to recognize any great imbalance and go forth into its very center, the place of the most unrest.

Here, as center, we will dance, sing and rejoice, for Divine Love is with us. Freedom is surely ours as we move fearlessly into the muck and mire of the night. It is only by conquering the fear in self that we conquer all evil.

Go forth with a mighty light and do what you know in Love's Name is right. Heaven's door awaits those who sing through the pain of the night.

~~~~

Each Little Step

It only takes a little step at a time, each little step moving forward and taking with it the creation of the greater self. You have seen to go forward and know it is the little step, flowing into the next, that makes creation possible.

You see the light and now you understand. You move forward with great honor and salute the power that gives you grace to carry on. There will be peace when you are done.

A light from the heart of God has sealed it with the Rainbow. Eternally Bowing, the One with you is now one with all.

~~~~

Legions of Light

Great glory and honor is pouring forth at this very moment as the grace of Divine Love, the True Consciousness, becomes manifest on earth.

The legions of light are now being accepted into the world of form as never before. Through these physical bodies, aligned with the universal truth, they can do mighty work.

Peace on earth, as a thought form, sweeps across the nations far and wide. The peace commanding presence of these, the most powerful, for they love the greatest, is bringing about "The Change."

The Garden Paradise of this sweet earth will be our Glory. As one, we bow in Divine Love and in Great Thanksgiving.

~~~~

~Day 108~
Best Day of My Life

Today will be the best day of my life. I will move forward into my supreme destiny for this life and day. I will not ponder, procrastinate or otherwise hesitate, but instead, move forward quickly into love that makes me whole.

I will, in short, not fear. I am in complete charge of my life and take control of all the stumbling blocks that come my way. God illumines my next step minute by minute and I am fully attuned to Love's will.

This is why today, like all days, will be the best day of my life. I am full of spiritual blessings and nothing can stand in my way as long as I "Love it Free."

The victory of living life to the fullest is mine and with humble gratitude I say, "I Love You."

~~~~

Heart of Hearts

Within my heart beats a still larger heart, the heart of hearts of all life. Indeed, it is the Heart of God, for we are all one. As my heart beats so beats all hearts and as they set forth their rhythm my heart attunes to them. We blend into the universal rhythm.

We now move forward with one heart, one mind and one hand and all of the illusory world falls away leaving the shinning light of reality. A smile from the face of Love, our true reality, brings us into Supreme Ecstasy.

The rhythm of the eternal cause is born into the eternal octave of light. We are joyful, happy and free. The harmony of our love brings us together as one.

~~~~

Three Freebirds

Awaiting now in the hearts of mankind is a nest that contains the three eggs of the Freebirds to come. In many of human these eggs have come forth and some have experienced the freedom coming from the heart can bring.

They find the first two Freebirds take flight and freedom is found in the *Mental* and *Physical* selves.

It is the Freebird of the complete trinity that brings forth the wonders of the Kingdom of Heaven. This Freebird is the one of Life Eternal found within the *Spiritual* being. It is the light that sustains all life.

Holy Trinity has now become one. The Freebird achieves its greatest message.

~~~~

~Day 111~
I, Like the Flower

Flowers with their beauty and fragrance grace my way this day. They sing a song of the time creation and I envisioned their message of truth and love. Elevated, my spirit is in harmony with nature's greatest secret of success; Beauty.

Now as I apply this beautiful essence to my being all are touched by my loving appearance and gentle waves of compassion. None can come my way and not feel my love for I, like the flower, give them ultimate freewill to accept me, yet my true beauty shines forth always.

By my grace they will know the truth of Love and will be set Free.

~~~~

I Am All Powerful

When I am feeling tired and weak, I will say, "Enough!" "I have had enough of your weeping and complaining, you, my physical body, for I am all powerful!"

When I am attuned to my higher self there is no pain, no blockages and no retreat. All works out in perfect accord. If it is my will it shall be done for Love Divine is my Comforter and I shall fear no evil.

In this Divine Love Consciousness all flows into the ultimate victory of success. It flows ever gently with all things.

It is only outside of this marvelous state the struggle begins. I set myself free this day and at every moment take charge of my life.

The wings of Mother/Father God are my reward.

~~~~

~Day 113~
We Are One

My hand extends out to you and touches you, as the dew touches the morning flower. In the comfort and solace of your soul I begin to realize you and I are one and the grace of Divine Source is what creates the connection.

We can now show our individuality and soar with great Freedom, while bowing to the single center; the Heart of Love Divine found in all creation. What a gift it is to have ultimate freedom, yet be joined in perfect union with you and all life.

My heart sings praises of Thanksgiving. Awaken, my child, from your slumber and extend your hand toward the Tree of Life. Now you can have the greatest freedom of all; Love.

~~~~

~Day 114~
The Immaculate Concept

Peace, the greatest reward for any striving, is now manifesting in the hearts and minds of the people as never before. Millions, indeed billions, are discovering what it is to love their brother and sister unconditionally.

This mighty surge of Love/Light is bringing about a radiant glow to this planet. The immaculate concept of Freedom's Holy Star is becoming the way we move with great strength into the New Age.

Peace, yes, sweet glorious peace, shall be our reward. The hungry shall be feed as the fountains of Living Waters pour forth on all life.

The true nature of Love and Light will be known and mankind will come together as one. The bowing has begun.

~~~~

~Day 115~
Joy In Every Facet

As we smile upon the hardships that come our way we receive a new sense of hope and enthusiasm. It is the one who is greatest who can remain joyful in the most trying situations.

Follow the example of those who express this joy in every facet of their life, for they will show you the nature of God.

Have respect for the Pure Ones who do not blemish their being with anything less than pure love and truth. A great gift is ours as we live in the joyful essence of purity.

All pain and strife will float on past, just as a gentle river carries the petal of the flower. Take heed to these words for it is in Joy freedom can be ours.

Sing your song today.

~~~~

Infinite Well of Love

Deep at the center of my being there is an infinite well of love. I sit silently and feel this love pulsating within me and suddenly the all-encompassing pulse of the universe is in rhythm with my pulsation of Love.

We are now one heart, controlled by omnipotent intelligence. I watch as I silently invoke this Love to nourish all life. It springs forth from my being and gently caresses all life.

They feel this love and are reborn. The infinite creative source of my being, in tune with Mother/Father God, has brought eternal life to all. Oh, the glory of it; life eternal conceived in love.

The great cosmic plan is now known and waves of Thanksgiving flow forth.

~~~~

~Day 117~
Illumine My Way

From my heart center I bring forth a light to illumine my way as I go on. Those who come in contact with my expression will feel a sense of inner peace and delight and thus take on a greater light themselves.

Love will rule the World!! This is the greatest expression anyone can make and now as we say, "I Love You." From the depths of our souls, our souls become one soul, one with the soul and the heart of Divine Presence.

What glories abound when the Human family truly love one another. The joy people are feeling inside becomes manifest and instantly the world is transformed into the Garden Paradise.

Heaven and earth in perfect accord. In truth, Love is the answer.

~~~~

~Day 118~
One With Angels

Closer and closer we draw to the time when the angels will sing, "Joy, Joy to the earth, for now you have become one with us." The true essence of the Divine in man has burst forward, through the veil, into light eternal.

The great self within found the key of Love and in truth used it for all life. The Harmony among all people is ever rejuvenated by the giving Mother/Father God and no longer is there death. We are truly one.

A singing of the soul of human with the greatest orchestration is now made manifest. "All for one and one for all," their voices sing.

Heaven's Glory is within our hearts. Oh, the glorious wonder of it.

~~~~

~Day 119~
Honest In All Ways

The victory of being truthful is one of the greatest, for it is by being truthful we are in alignment with the universe. Who ever heard of nature telling a lie?

It is only the human race who lies, for they are the only ones given a choice to believe the illusion or the reality. We have freewill. This is why we can work our way back to the heart of God. When we do Divine Source's will we are in tune with nature and therefore honest.

To truly be a part of the all-encompassing field we must be honest in All ways, especially to ourselves, not letting fear guide our lives.

As we salute the truth in all nature and live it we become one with it and with Mother/Father God. Truth brought into harmony with love is the greatest victory.

~~~~

Divine Mother and Father

In exultation I look to the Mother and see Her goodness as Her creation is brought into being. Gently I float with Her creative spirit and I am now a creator too.

We join as one, ever nurtured by the Father. His presence is what brings forth the joy and beauty I am now perfectly flowing with.

The two sparks, the Divine Mother and Father, sing a glorious song together. Now we see the light of love illuminating the creation and instantly we are transmuted into a divine being by this essence of perfection.

What a gift the creative flow is and, as we share it, we know it is the most powerful source in the universe.

~~~~

~Day 121~
Saints of Peace

What a beautiful day this is, for you are in my life. There are saints in my life who have shown me the way through the darkness and now all I see is light.

You and I are one with these Saints of Peace, for we love. They have kindled a mighty flame in our heart.

Truly from the wisdom they share we can all say, "Divine Presence, make us instruments of your peace. Where there is fear, let me sow love."

Thank you for being you. Now on the wings of silver you have given me, I Fly, I Love and the Message of God is in my hand. I love you Saints of Peace for we are one.

~~~~

~Day 122~
Highest and Best Guidance

Thank you Divine Presence for showing me the way today. I know as I look out, with my eyes in attunement, I will see the guidance being sent me.

This guidance, from the heavenly realm will be of the highest and best; saluting the one life that lives in all. The victory is ours as we attune to the divine message.

The Light and Love, from us and the all-encompassing, will be the only path for it is our greatest desire to serve Love Divine and bring forth Love's word in every expression of our being.

It is from this pure expression we will be guided into light and love supreme. It is the greatest gift of all to be in loving communication with all life.

~~~~

Love and Truth Balance

The balance between love and truth is an ultimate state of being. We must accept what we see in the full light of consciousness and then bring it into the full glory of manifestation through the love that pours into our being.

This love is ours and it is the Mother/Father God's and it is unconditional. The science of who this is will bring this nature of God to full illumination and therein the universal spirituality will seal this reality in divine love.

Grace, Strength, Hope and Beauty will radiate from any and all as they send forth this mighty gift of love and truth and we will be free.

The Masters smile with joy.

~~~~

Twinkle in Your Eyes

Peace, Peace be unto you my child. Let me dry away your tears that I may see your loving and gentle smile again. The days of happiness are here today but there are still some who can trip you up, causing you to fall and once again the roughness of this earth is experienced.

I ask you, my child, to not curse those for they act out of confusion. Smile on them and with that twinkle in your eyes they, too, will become a Child of the Divine. Come to know of the greatest source in the universe; come to know love

You, my Divine Child, have such a gift in who you are. Your innocence lights my way and the laughter you share brings joy to my soul. May Divine Source bless you and keep you.

~~~~

~Day 125~
Bowing to Center

Beloved and mighty victorious presence I am. I bow to the center within me and the center within all life. The love , the creating and sustaining factor of the universe, is in tune with the rhythm I set forth.

All of life is singing with one voice and in perfect harmony. Human Divine and God become one in the pure essence of joy and the flowing gift of the Healing Waters is our victory... Hallelujah, Hallelujah; Praise be to Mother/Father God.

The beauty of the greatest flower radiates in the smiles of those who say, "I Am." They have joined heart, hand and mind for peace and the permanent Garden of heaven on earth is the reward of Grace.

~~~~

~Day 126~
United Being

Yes, it all does work together in perfect order. Those with ears to hear and eyes to see know we are all connected beings.

My Love, as the Rainbow is seven-fold then so are we. Know the wisdom in this and it will set you Free. The Masters know of the truth found in Uniting our States of Being. They, as you can and will, unite Divine Will in perfect intonation and connect All; Mother/Father God, Love and Divine Presence.

Success in all ventures is now realized and the joy of love is here to stay.

Hear You People from all walks of life; The message and the covenant is in the Rainbow. Look with your mind and heart as one and you will see. You, too, will Bow to the Divine Creative Source.

~~~~

~Day 127~
You are the Creator

Let the grace of Divine Presence be with you. Smile at its creation and its creation will smile back at you. Begin to experience the life that gives you control of all outside influences.

Rest within on the pillow of Love and know it is the gentleness of the spirit you carry to all life that brings you the greatest strength.

Love, love and love some more. Take your power from within and connect it with the universal flow of Love and Wisdom.

You are now the Creator and all of heaven and earth are at your command. You serve all creation and it serves you. Relaxed, you simply know, "How Great Love IS."

~~~~

~Day 128~
Nature's Greatest Miracle

Bring joy to the world and the beauty of the world will be yours. Find peace within your soul and never will the anguish of war effect you.

Know of Love and you will be protected with the greatest of shields and you will hold the key to the hearts of all mankind. You are nature's greatest miracle.

Sing and joy will fill your being. Dance to the sound of sweet music in your life and the rhythm between you and Divine Source will flow. Be of Joyful Nature, my friend, for this lights the minds and hearts of all you touch.

With Joy, Love will be with you every step of the way. The greatest beauty and joy is found when one is in tune with the Joy of God.

~~~~

~Day 129~
Holy Pure Love

Rejoice People of the Earth! Now you have been shown to the light of what is right. Reach forth in the full dominion of your Holy Pure Love and be the Light to the world you truly are, for Divine Presence is within.

You have chosen good over evil, light over darkness and the victory of eternal life. You are Free.

Rejoice, knowing your Holy, Pure and Just self is the key to the Rainbow Bridge. Take hold, for in your hand is the key of the heart. It is the salvation of all who seek peace, contentment and happiness. Take charge in love and truth.

~~~~

~Day 130~
Master is Example

One must at times endure the struggles and harshness living the 3D experience can bring us. Not only for self must this be done, but also for the glorious self of all mankind.

All must come to know, " It is not the life you live, but the courage in which you live it." The greatest name for Master is "Example." As your example goes forth in full dominion, conquering all strife, Know that you are the light of the world.

Come forth fearlessly and carry the banner of love and freedom home. Come to God for Divine Creation's home is where the heart is. Follow yours today and you will always be Happy, Joyous and Free.

~~~~

~Day 131~
Love's Mercy

Let the grace of the Living Mother/Father God be there with you and Know, "Divine Source is my Shepherd, I shall not want." Know of the truth that more than a thousand times one can fall to the dust and if they pick their selves up yet one more time God will extend a loving arm.

Know there are Masters whose sole purpose is to dust off the fallen ones who ask for help. Seek Love Divine and all else shall be added.

The grace of God is truly miraculous for within burns a mighty flame of salvation for all. Feel love for all and you too will be in utmost grace.

Praise be to God for Love's mercy sets the captives Free.

~~~~

~Day 132~
This Beautiful Child

Awaken the small child within you and live the innocence, beauty and tenderheartedness found in those formative years. In truth, this is the true nature of our being. It was only our fear based attachments that brought about the things and experiences less than this beautiful child.

Now go forth into the world for everybody loves a lover. Now find your talent, pursue it and bring this light of the child to all you touch.

The victory awaits those of humble nature who illumine within the glorious light of God. Follow the Masters and it shall be yours. Awaken within, my child, and become one with the ocean of Living Love.

~~~~

~Day 133~
Wings of an Eagle

With the wings of an Eagle I set myself free this day. I now move this eagle into my heart and these wings take on the dimensions found in God.

With Love truly I can fly in the heart center of all life as the Divine Mother/Father God does. Great peace extends over my being and all I come in contact with it, for freedom is radiating forth and the victory of love and truth is at hand.

I accept it and fly mightily, yet ever so gently into more life streams. In acceptance, I have a greater field of influence over the laws that govern people's perception.

They accept God's will and we All Fly Free.

~~~~

~Day 134~
Intimate Connection

Oh wonderful and glorious Master. You have come the way before me and know of the laws of Love and Truth. Guide my way as I venture out into this earth plane.

Rest your hand in my hand and through your intimate connection with the field show me through God's creation the path that is right.

Thank you, Wonderful Master, for being the Example you are, ever living in the light. You have lit my heart center and I too can be this Example/Master.

Many feel my light of love and are nourished by it for you and I are one. In the reality of love there is no competition, only sharing and caring with all life for life. So Be It.

~~~~

~Day 135~
Fly Freely

Let your spirit know; God is in you. You must fly freely into all places your Holy-Self pulls you. Know of the good and dwell only in the reality. By and by you will learn the lessons of the Masters before you.

Fly gracefully even in the most trying situations. Alive and awake you will bring forth revelation those among you need to hear.

Attune your ear to your fellowman for Divine Source works through Its creation. It is in giving and receiving from the heart we are doubly blessed.

Find your light within and share Alls light within and receive. Freedom Awaits!!

~~~~

Heart's Secret Chamber

Go within that secret chamber of your heart and discover the most powerful energy in the world. Know that your operation from the heart center is not only of your self but also of the greater self.

All central focuses, the heart center, is in tune with every other heart center. Rejoice for this center of centers is of the greatest miracles of all. It gives the Masters all power in heaven and earth, and it,too, is your heritage .

Take heart, one with all hearts, and the glorious victory shall be yours. Now the time is at hand. Be the lover of all life you truly are and bring God Love/Light/Life into all the world.

~~~~

~Day 137~
My Next Step

As I move forward I begin to see exactly what my next step is. Divine Source moves upon the point of Its central focus and the light of Awareness brings about the creation.

Divine Love, let me be an instrument of your peace. As I focus out toward a next step, direct my eyes, hands, heart and mind that it be the greatest step; the step that serves all life.

Let it be the step the Master would take. Let love be the conquering presence of all woes.

Within all creation there is a focus of the highest and best. With true love I know it can be reached. Within the heart center Peace will manifest.

~~~~

~Day 138~
Perfect Communication

Signs and wonders are all around for the person who simply opens their eyes and sees the connections. In truth, all points in the universe are in perfect communication with all other points.

Awaken to this truth and set yourself free. The answers you seek are always right there. As you apply your being in love and truth, the foundation stone the universe is built upon, you will receive and generate the ultimate communication; beyond time and place.

Oh, what wonders can take place in the universal state. Apply your being and float gently down the river of life. Heaven awaits you.

~~~~

~Day 139~
Mother Earth Father Sky

Awaken you people from all walks of life and know of Mother Earth, for she loves you unconditionally. She will always bring forth her highest and best message to guide you into the ways of the spirit; the spirit in tune with Father Sky.

Together these two ultimate sparks of creation join and life is now manifest. Be one with the flow. Stand without fear or disbelief in Their center and sing with joy.

In your joy all things are attuned with the Mother-Father spark and will respond perfectly to your commanding presence, for They love you. Love, give and receive.

~~~~

Come All One Together

Come all you brothers and sisters. Come all, one together. Feel that joy. Feel that bliss, spread that smile around.

Give this joy, bliss and inner truth to all you see along your way down your journey of life. A life of good nature will be good with you, for as you are in the spirit the spirit of nature flows with your natural state.

Let your natural state be of what is good, pure and just and never will you lack. All is given to the ones in nature for they are one with Divine Source.

Awakened, I give the gift of the word and become the Freebird.

~~~~

~Day 141~
Giving Our Love

Within the heart of every man, woman and child is a deep sense of wanting to give. They see those who hunger, are homeless and live in bondage. They wish they could make a change, but how?

A focus needs to arise within this center of love and its flame needs to go forth. Carry the banner of love forth great children of light. Hold it high for all to see.

It is in giving our love we see it return. We must put forth if we hope to make a change. Feel at peace, as a mighty lion, and go as a king into the jungle of society.

Free yourself and with love you will free them.

~~~~

~Day 142~
Bare Your Light

Give life a chance, for it is the strength found within the heart that carries the mighty banner of light on. Become focused on this reality and bare your light for all to follow.

Go through the darkness of those who do not understand. Radiate your greatest power; Your Love-Light. Give Freely and give in abundance. You are full of power and bring a spark of happiness in all expression.

Now Free, you fly and all others are free to fly too.   You elevate them and in the light of righteousness evermore is accomplished.

~~~~

~Day 143~
Peace, My Rainbow

Let your focus be on what is pure, holy and just. Let this pure essence guide you into all walks and talks of life.

The creation of the world around you is in your hands. Will you reach out and take hold? Find peace in the end of the rainbow which starts from a single white light and goes into a beautiful spectrum of many colors.

See this and apply it to your life. Nature works perfectly for happiness, you can too. Find the focus between the one and the all and with joy sing forth a happy tune with the Creator.

At last, Peace, my rainbow of great beauty.

~~~~

Freedom's Greatest Gift

Freedom is the greatest gift of all and yet it is the one that provides us with the hardest lessons until we learn its real meaning. Come forth and see freedom in this way; "One for all and all for one." This is the golden key to freedom.

If an exclusion is taking place on any level it blocks freedom, for freedom is all-encompassing. Be Free and take this word to those in bondage. Love them, Love them Free.

Love and freedom are one. As one with them your life will be filled with Joy. Joy is God's nature. Find it and you will have freedom. Live in joy and you will show your love for all life.

~~~~

~Day 145~
Way to the Light

In the ways of spirit there is a foundation stone that comes as a mighty lesson to you; "Keep Up."

Discouragement may knock against your door, yet you know the way to the light, for at the end of the tunnel, no matter how long and rugged, there is a light.

We must Keep Up if we are to be victorious. Find that flicker of light and feel its love drawing you ever forward. One step at a time, one more time you go into the unknown.

By Keeping Up you will make it. Believe this; know this and it will set you free from the daily drudgery and your eyes will soon see sweet peace.

Keep Up and all good things will come.

~~~~

~Day 146~
Love Divine's Banner

One could say we are a day late and the message no longer has its place. One could say we must start over. Yet we, the Light Bearers for Love Divine, carry our banner of truth and love high.

It lights our way wherever we go and is not contained in finite time It is present beyond all time. Beyond time, we are in spirit. Our message goes to exactly the place it needs to be. It is in perfect accord.

So carry that banner on, your word, your truth and the way to life. These are gifts to be shared with all and the spirit you carry with you determines its destination.

Above all, "Love." This is the golden key to the message and now its truth will reign supreme.

~~~~

~Day 147~
Key to Peace

So you say you want to be a spiritual warrior and fight the injustices of the world? Go forth, dear one, yet do not forget your sword of truth. Carry this high in all the situations you venture into.

Know it is by seeing the truth that conquers the "beast," for the beast thrives in darkness and illusion. It is your power within that brings about the victory.

The most powerful one of all is the one who loves the most. With the sword of truth and a shield of love no evil can stand its ground against you.

This is the key to peace on this troubled earth. Go forth noble one and carry your banner high.

~~~~

~Day 148~
Path I Choose

What a glorious day this is for today I see what path I wish to choose. The way ahead of me is lit and becomes brighter with each step I take.

It is in the moving forward that I find the right way. The Master always moves forward and so shall I. I know I want peace for all life, yet this peace must be found within. I accept it now!!

I see the restlessness of a troubled world and yet only feel peace, joy and love. This is a way to peace.

In great communion I fly into the heart of Divine Source, the heart of all hearts. Here the I Am presence is all. I bow to heart center and the way of peace is found.

~~~~

~Day 149~
The New Song

Each day is a special gift and we should be thankful for within this day is life. Thank Divine Source for Its being, in which we move and have our being, sustaining all the infinite beauties of creation.

We as co-creators, see the greatness of this life and we are born anew. We can now sing the new, new song and waves of thanksgiving pour from our soul. We now choose in complete freewill to be of service to all mankind, indeed, all life.

We affirm at every step, "I love you and want you to be happy, joyous and free," then stand back and let Love do Its mighty work.

Thank You God for your Gift of Life.

~~~~

Rainbow Peace Bridge

Peace and blessing be to you, my Beloved. You have shown me to the way of dancing in the flowers.

God is truly burning within you and your peaceful way brings me to great contentment. We have came as one, from crawl, to walk, to run.

Now we fly and the grace of the spirit shines gently into all. We fly for creativity and all involved see eye to eye.

Thank you for the child in you brings the child in me forth. A Bridge of the Rainbow Peace Puzzle is now ready to be crossed and we take into our arms the way of Love.

Yes, Love is the Way.

~~~~

12184567R00087

Made in the USA
Charleston, SC
18 April 2012